Pet Care

Puppies

Rebecca Sjonger & Bobbie Kalman

Photographs by Marc Crabtree

🌱 Crabtree Publishing Company

www.crabtreebooks.com

Puppies

A Bobbie Kalman Book

Dedicated by Heather Fitzpatrick
To Gloria Nesbitt and her favorite furry friend Dawson

Editor-in-Chief
Bobbie Kalman

Writing team
Rebecca Sjonger
Bobbie Kalman

Substantive editor
Kathryn Smithyman

Editors
Amanda Bishop
Kelley MacAulay

Art director
Robert MacGregor

Design
Margaret Amy Reiach

Production coordinator
Heather Fitzpatrick

Photo research
Crystal Foxton

Consultant
Dr. Michael A. Dutton, DVM, DABVP, Weare Animal Hospital,
www.weareanimalhospital.com

Special thanks to
Jeremy Payne, Dave Payne, Shelbi Setikas, Bailee Setikas, Arunas
Setikas, Sheri Setikas, Gloria Nesbitt, Lateesha Warner, Connie
Warner, Nancy Richards and Healey, Jeannette Thompson and
Emma, Michelle Hagar, John Hagar and Buckley, Rose Gowsell,
Gary Pattison and Tank, Kathy Middleton, Vanessa Diodatti

Photographs
John Daniels/ardea.com: page 13 (top)
Marc Crabtree: front cover, pages 1, 4, 5, 14, 15 (top & middle), 16,
    18, 19 (bottom), 20, 21 (brushes), 22, 24, 25, 28, 29 (bottom), 30, 31
Bobbie Kalman: page 7 (bottom)
Other images by PhotoDisc, Comstock, and Adobe Image Library

Illustrations
Barbara Bedell: pages 26, 27
Margaret Amy Reiach: page 17

Digital prepress
Embassy Graphics

Printer
Worzalla Publishing Company

Crabtree Publishing Company

www.crabtreebooks.com   1-800-387-7650

PMB 16A	612 Welland Avenue	73 Lime Walk
350 Fifth Avenue	St. Catharines	Headington
Suite 3308	Ontario	Oxford
New York, NY	Canada	OX3 7AD
10118	L2M 5V6	United Kingdom

Cataloging-in-Publication Data
Sjonger, Rebecca.
  Puppies / Rebecca Sjonger & Bobbie Kalman;
photographs by Marc Crabtree.
    p. cm. -- (Pet care series)
  Includes index.
  ISBN 0-7787-1751-8 (RLB) -- ISBN 0-7787-1783-6 (pbk.)
  1. Puppies--Juvenile literature. 2. Dogs--Juvenile literature.
[1. Dogs. 2. Animals--Infancy. 3. Pets.] I. Kalman, Bobbie.
II. Crabtree, Marc, ill. III. Title. IV. Series.
  SF426.5.S57 2004
  636.7'07--dc22
                                                      2003024978
                                                      LC

Contents

What are puppies? 4

The right pet for you? 6

Dozens of dogs 8

Newborns 10

Picking your puppy 12

Welcome home! 14

Bow-wow chow 16

Housebreaking 18

Pampered pooch 20

Training tips 22

Play time 24

Getting the message 26

Staying safe 28

Visiting a vet 30

Words to know and Index 32

What are puppies?

Puppies are young dogs. Dogs are **mammals**. Mammals are animals that have backbones. Like all mammals, puppies have fur or hair on their bodies. Mother mammals make milk inside their bodies to feed their babies.

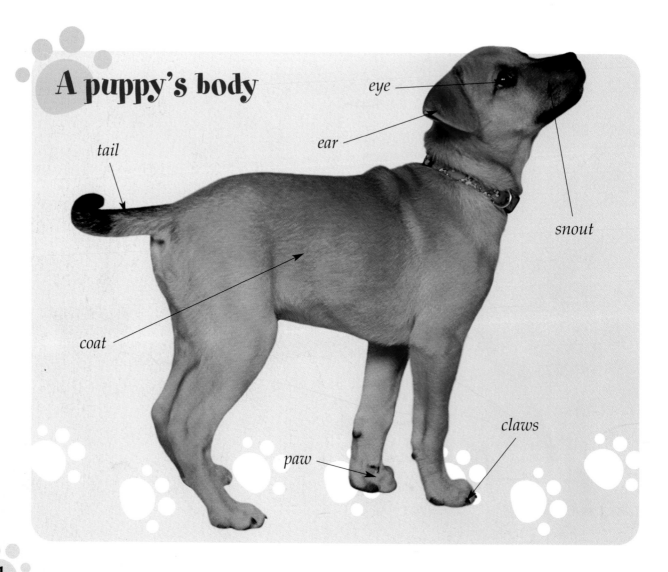

A puppy's body

eye

ear

snout

tail

coat

paw

claws

Wild wolves

Pet dogs are related to wolves. Wolves live and hunt for food in **packs**, or groups. Long ago, some wolves were tamed by people. After many years, these wolves became pet dogs. Today, dogs need people to feed and care for them.

The family this dog lives with is its pack!

The right pet for you?

Puppies are popular pets because they are cute, loyal, and fun. Taking good care of a puppy can be a lot of work, though! You and your family will have to feed and walk your pet and play with it every day. Puppies also need to be **trained** and **groomed**, or cleaned.

You will be your pet's best friend!

A dog's life

Your puppy will be part of your family for a long time. Most dogs live from six to sixteen years. As your dog grows older, you will still need to love it and look after it every day.

Are you ready?

Before you decide to get a puppy, get your family together and answer the questions below.

- Who will feed it every day?

- Will you train your puppy to be **housebroken** and clean up its messes?

- Will you have time to groom your puppy?

- Will you spend at least ten minutes every day training your puppy to behave?

- Do you have time to walk your puppy and play with it?

- A dog can cost a lot of money each year. Is your family prepared to pay for food and special care?

- Is anyone in your family **allergic** to dogs?

Dozens of dogs

Dogs come in many sizes, colors, and shapes. There are hundreds of **breeds**, or kinds, of pet dogs. Dogs of the same breed look and act the same. **Purebred** dogs have parents and grandparents from the same breed. A purebred puppy will grow up to be like its parents. You will know how it will look and act as an adult dog. Some of the most popular breeds are shown on these pages.

Labrador Retrievers are big, strong dogs. They are friendly family pets.

German Shepherds are very smart. Police often use them on missions!

Dachshunds are very active. Their long bodies are shaped like wieners. Some people call them "wiener dogs!"

Golden Retrievers like to have fun! These dogs need a lot of space for running and playing.

Mixed breeds

Mongrel, or mixed-breed, dogs have parents and grandparents from more than one breed. It is hard to tell what they will be like as adult dogs. They make great pets, though! Mongrels are friendly and healthy. They are also less expensive to buy than purebred dogs.

Newborns

Puppies are born in **litters**, or groups, of up to twelve puppies. **Newborn**, or baby, puppies are very small. When they are born, they are not able to see or hear. Most puppies open their eyes for the first time when they are about two weeks old. They can hear soon after that.

When your puppy is around one month old, it will start playing with its brothers and sisters. You can play with the puppies then, too!

Time with Mom

A puppy needs time with its mother before it can come to live with your family. Your puppy must stay with its mother until it is eight to eleven weeks old. Then it will be old enough to leave its family and join yours!

Picking your puppy

To find a puppy, ask **veterinarians**, friends, or your local **animal shelter** if they know of any that are being given away. You can also buy your puppy from a **breeder** or pet store. Make sure you get your pet from people who take very good care of their dogs and puppies.

What to look for

You will probably pick a playful, friendly puppy. Make sure it is also healthy! Choose a puppy that has:

- clear, alert eyes
- clean, shiny ears with no wax inside
- a clean snout, behind, and coat
- no **fleas**, sores, or scratches on its skin

The most playful puppy may also be the one that takes the most work to train!

Growing quickly

Your puppy will grow up to be a dog in about one year. Before you pick a puppy, find out what size it will be when it is fully grown. Large dogs need more space, exercise, and food than small dogs need. Do you have enough space in your home for a fully grown dog?

An adult Chihuahua may weigh less than six pounds (2.7 kg).

This Bernese Mountain Dog puppy may weigh 100 pounds (45 kg) when it is fully grown!

Welcome home!

Before you bring your puppy home, make sure you have everything you need to take care of it properly.

Your puppy needs a bowl for food and a bowl for water.

collar

leash

Put a **collar** on your puppy before taking it outdoors. A **leash** will help you keep your pet from running away.

bristle brush

wire brush

You need a brush to groom your puppy's coat.

Choose a few different toys for your puppy to play with.

Naptime

Puppies need a lot of sleep. You can make a small bed from a cardboard box or you can buy a pet bed. Put it in a quiet corner of your home. Make sure your family and friends leave your puppy alone when it is sleeping!

Your puppy may sleep better if it hears the sound of a ticking clock. Tuck one into its bed.

Settling in

When you first bring your new puppy home, it may be scared. It needs to get used to you and your family. Be very patient and gentle. Soon your puppy will want to play and explore!

Bow-wow chow

Ask your pet's veterinarian or "vet" about healthy brands of dog food. He or she can also tell you how much to feed your pet as it grows. Until they are six months old, puppies need to be fed three to four times a day. Older dogs need to be fed only once or twice each day.

canned food

dry food

Dry food and *canned food* can both be very healthy for your puppy. Dry food stays fresh longer, though.

Fresh water

Your puppy will need fresh water in a bowl. Keep the bowl filled with water all day long! Be sure to clean your puppy's food and water bowls every day.

Fresh water is all your pet needs to drink.

People food

Be very careful if you give anything other than dog food to your puppy or dog!

- You may give your puppy bite-sized chunks of cooked beef. Never give it a bone! Your puppy may choke on it.

- Eating **dairy foods** such as milk or ice cream can make your puppy sick.

- Never feed your puppy raw meat or eggs!

- Even a small amount of chocolate can make your puppy very ill.

Housebreaking

Teach your puppy when and where it can go to the bathroom. This training is called "housebreaking." You must be **consistent**, or regular, with the training. If you repeat the same actions over and over, your puppy will soon learn what you want it to do. Remember to be patient while the puppy is learning!

You can protect the floors of your home with newspapers while you are housebreaking your puppy.

Let me out!

Most dogs will need to go to the bathroom ten to twenty minutes after drinking water. When this time has passed, attach your dog's leash to its collar and walk it to a good spot outdoors. Use the same spot every time to help your puppy remember what to do. Praise your puppy when it has finished. Wait until afterward to play with your puppy.

Your pet will get your attention when it needs to go out. Watch for any warning signs and take it out right away!

Keep it clean

If your puppy has had an accident in your home, wash the area right away. Wipe the floor with vinegar or a "pet accident" spray, or your pet will go again to the same spot.

Pampered pooch

Your puppy will be happy and healthy when you take good care of it. Make time every week to groom your dog. An adult may have to help you with some of these jobs.

Clicky claws

If your puppy's claws are clicking on the floor, they are too long. Ask your veterinarian to show you how to cut the hooked ends of the puppy's claws with special clippers.

Terrific teeth

Crunchy food and hard toys help keep your puppy's teeth and gums clean and healthy. You can also brush your pet's teeth with toothpaste made just for dogs.

Grooming your dog

Brushing is an important part of grooming your pet. Slowly pull the brush along your dog's body. Check for **matted**, or tangled, fur as you brush. Gently untangle the fur with your fingers. Also check if your puppy's ears are dirty. Dogs with long fur on their ears may need your help keeping them clean. Wipe the outside of the ears with a damp towel. As you groom your puppy, look for fleas on its skin.

Long-haired dogs need to be brushed every other day. Use a wire brush and be very gentle.

Short-haired dogs should be brushed once a week with a bristle brush.

Training tips

Your puppy needs you to teach it how to behave. Training may take a long time. Be patient! Trained adult dogs are happy and well behaved. Spend ten to twenty minutes every day teaching your puppy. Train it how to behave in your home as well as outdoors.

Basic commands

Begin training your puppy with **commands**, or instructions, such as "sit" or "stay." First, show it what you want it to do. For example, gently guide your puppy to sit down while saying "sit." Praise it and give it a treat after it is sitting. Repeat this many times. Soon your puppy will sit down whenever you say "sit." Praise it every time!

Good boy!

Your pet wants to please you. Always praise it when it behaves. Never hit or yell at your puppy, or it will become afraid of you. Have some fun with your puppy after training. It will then look forward to training with you!

You can train your puppy to do fun things, too. This dog is going to "shake hands!"

Dog school

By the time your puppy is six months old, it should know some basic commands. It is then time to go to **obedience school**, or a school for training dogs. A good trainer will show you how to get your puppy to obey you. You and your puppy will learn many commands.

Play time

Spend around a half hour every day having some fun with your puppy. Regular exercise will keep both of you feeling great! Puppies love playing games. Try playing different games with yours and find out what it enjoys. Many puppies like playing fetch with a Frisbee, a stick, or a ball. Some puppies will even play hide-and-seek with you!

Your puppy will be excited to play with you!

Fun run

Most dogs need to go for a walk or run at least once a day. After your puppy has had its first visit with a veterinarian, it can go outside on a leash. Only let your dog off its leash if you are in an area with a fence.

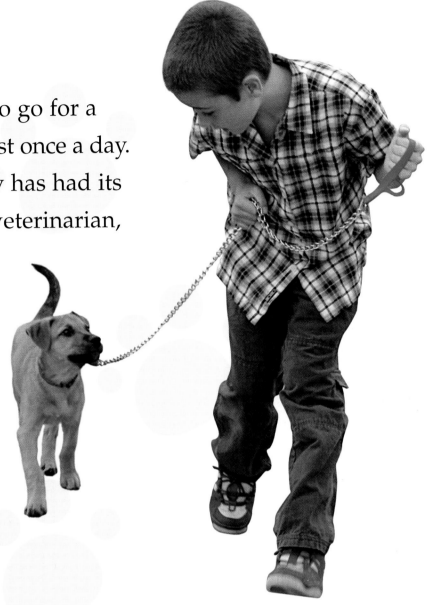

Safe return

When your dog is outdoors, it must wear a tag showing your name and address on its collar. If your dog gets lost, it will then be returned to you. In some areas, it is against the law for your dog not to wear a collar with an identification tag!

Getting the message

Your puppy will send messages to people and other animals. Dogs make sounds that let others know how they are feeling. Your puppy may bark when it is excited, growl when it is threatened, or howl when it is lonely. Dogs also use **body language** to show how they feel. They move their ears, mouths, and tails in ways that express their feelings.

This dog is raising its ears. It is curious about something it sees.

*This dog is hanging its head and is pulling back its gums. This behavior shows that it is **submissive**. When a dog is submissive, it lets you know that you are the boss!*

This dog has tucked its tail between its legs to show it is fearful and will be submissive.

This dog has raised its tail and is wagging it in the air. It is playful and excited!

Grrr!

A dog that is feeling threatened may stare at whatever has upset it. It may also show all its teeth and look scary. If your pet starts acting this way, it may be difficult for you to keep it under control. Tell an adult if your dog starts to be **aggressive**, or angry.

Staying safe

Respect your pet's **territory**, or personal space. One way a dog protects its space is by biting. If you disturb a dog while it is eating or try to take a toy away from it, you may be bitten. You should train your puppy to share its territory. This training will help keep other people safe when they are around your dog.

Tell your friends when they can pet your puppy and when they should leave it alone.

Be careful

A dog that is about to attack may warn you first. Be careful if it shows its teeth, growls, or flattens its ears. Stay as calm as you can if the dog attacks you. Do not look it in the eyes. Stand very still and say "no" in a firm voice. If you yell or try to run away, the dog may become more excited.

Dog fight!

If your puppy gets in a fight with another dog, do not try to separate the dogs. You could be hurt! Slowly back away and find an adult who can deal with the dogs.

Visiting a vet

As soon as you get your puppy, take it to a veterinarian. He or she will check the puppy for diseases. The puppy will also be given **vaccinations** with needles to keep it from being sick in the future. Take it to the vet every year for a regular check-up and vaccinations. Also think about having your puppy **neutered**. A neutered dog is not able to make puppies.

A veterinarian is a medical doctor who treats animals. He or she helps you keep your pet healthy.

Staying healthy

If your puppy ever gets sick or injured, take it to the veterinarian right away. Never give your puppy medicine that is meant for other animals or people! If you help it stay healthy, you and your dog will be together for a long time!

Get help

If your puppy vomits, faints, or limps, take it to the vet right away. Check its eyes, ears, and snout during grooming. If there is thick yellow fluid coming from any of these parts, your puppy needs to visit the vet. Other signs of illness are sleepiness, drinking a lot of water, and not eating the usual amount of food.

Words to know

Note: Boldfaced words that are defined in the book may not appear on this page.

allergic Describing someone who has a physical reaction to something such as a food or animal dander

animal shelter A center that houses and cares for animals that do not have owners

body language A type of communication that uses body movements to show feelings

breeder A person who brings dogs together so the dogs can make puppies

dairy foods Foods made with milk and milk products

fleas Tiny biting insects that live on the skin of animals

housebroken Describing an animal that is trained to relieve itself in the correct place

neuter To make an animal unable to make babies

train To teach an animal how to behave

vaccination A way of protecting a body against diseases

veterinarian A medical doctor who treats animals

Index

body language 26
breeds 8-9
claws 4, 20
coat 4, 12, 14
collar 14, 19, 25
commands 22, 23
ears 4, 12, 21 26, 29, 31
exercise 13, 24
eyes 4, 10, 12, 29, 31

food 5, 6, 7, 13, 14, 16-17, 20, 31
grooming 6, 7, 14, 20-21, 31
housebreaking 7, 18-19
leash 14, 19, 25
neutering 30
obedience school 23
playing 6, 7, 9, 10, 14, 15, 19, 24-25

purebreds 8, 9
safety 28-29
snout 4, 12, 31
tail 4, 26, 27
teeth 20, 27, 29
training 6, 7, 12, 18, 22-23, 28
veterinarian 12, 16, 20, 25, 30-31
walking 6, 7, 25

1 2 3 4 5 6 7 8 9 0 Printed in the U.S.A. 3 2 1 0 9 8 7 6 5 4